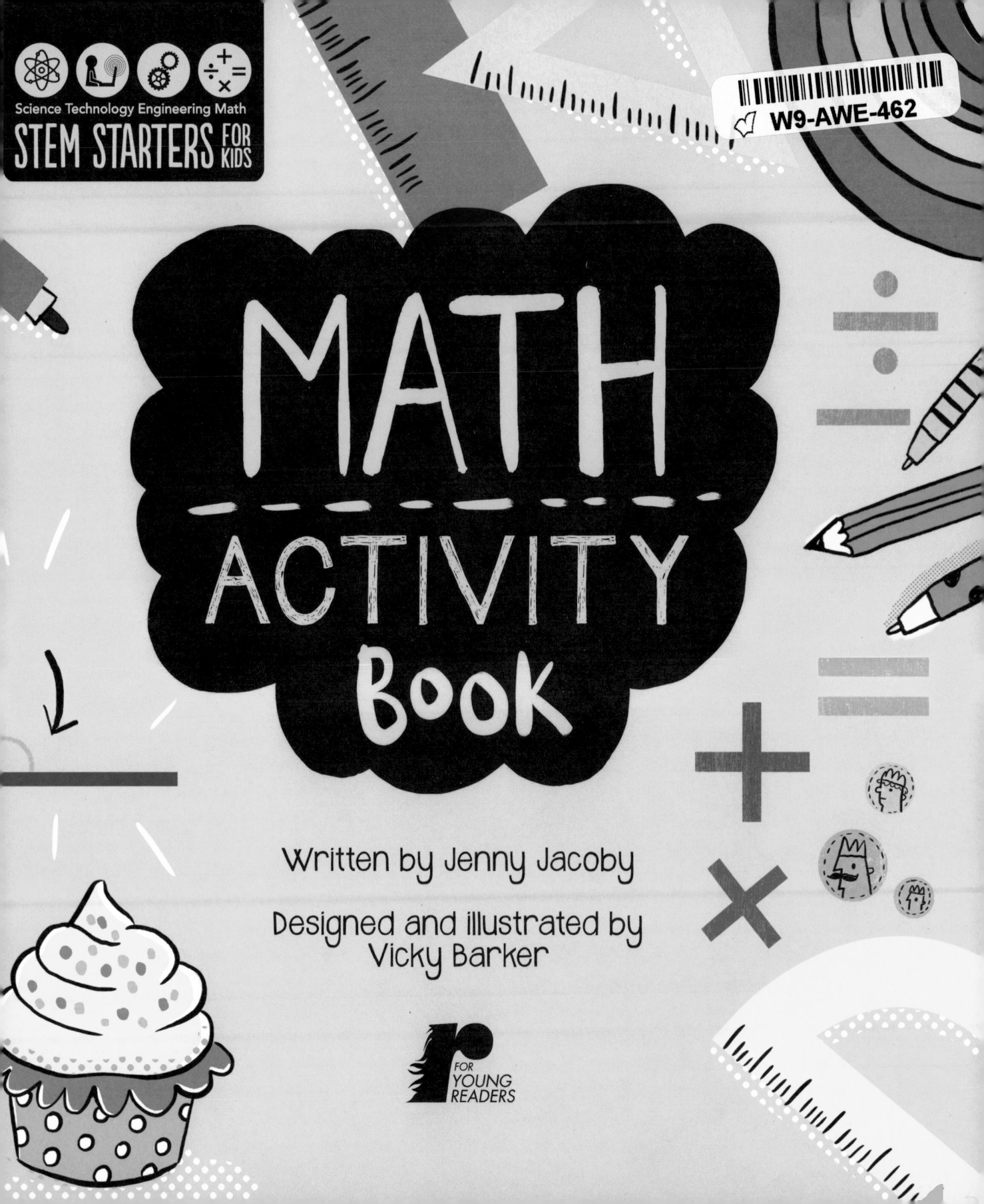
Science Technology Engineering Math
STEM STARTERS FOR KIDS
W9-AWE-462
MATH
ACTIVITY
Book
Written by Jenny Jacoby
Designed and illustrated by
Vicky Barker
FOR YOUNG READERS

Copyright © 2016
bsmall publishing ltd.

First Racehorse for Young Readers Edition 2017

All rights reserved. No part of this book may be reproduced in any manner without the express written consent of the publisher, except in the case of brief excepts in critical reviews or articles. All inquiries should be addressed to Racehorse for Young Readers, 307 West 36th Street, 11th Floor, New York, NY 10018.

Racehorse for Young Readers books may be purchased in bulk at special discounts for sales promotions, corporate gifts, fund-raising or education purposes. Special editions can also be created to specifications. For details, contact the Special Sales Department at Racehorse for Young Readers, 307 West 36th Street, 11th Floor, New York, NY 10018 or info@skyhorsepublishing.com.

Racehorse for Young Readers™ is a pending trademark of Skyhorse Publishing, Inc.®, a Delaware corporation.

Visit our website at skyhorsepublishing.com

10 9 8 7 6 5 4 3

Printed in China

ISBN
978-1-63158-193-9

WHAT IS MATH?

Math is more than just adding up, taking away, multiplying and dividing. Math is more than just numbers! Math is part of everybody's daily life, from spending money and checking your change, to following a recipe correctly—even finding patterns in the world and sharing properly with your friends.

WHAT IS STEM?

STEM stands for "science, technology, engineering and mathematics." These four areas are closely linked: new discoveries in science give technology and engineering new things to invent to make our lives easier and the world a better place. However, you could say that mathematics is the most important one as no scientist or engineer could do their job properly without it!

Science

Technology

Engineering

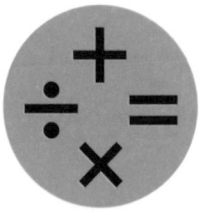

Math

MEASURING AND GUESSING

There are lots of ways to measure lengths. You can use a ruler or tape measure to measure accurately, or you can estimate—which is a bit like clever guessing. Estimating takes practice but there are some tricks to help you.

Symbols

=

This sign means "equal to" and is used when measuring accurately.

≈

This sign means "approximately equal to" and is used when estimating measurements.

Take a look at these shapes and use the guide to estimate their sizes. The pencils and tomatoes are the correct size on the page so you can use a ruler to check your estimate.

Guide

1 cm ≈ the width of a pencil

3 cm ≈ the length of a cherry tomato

1 m ≈ the width of a single bed

2 m ≈ the height of a door in a house

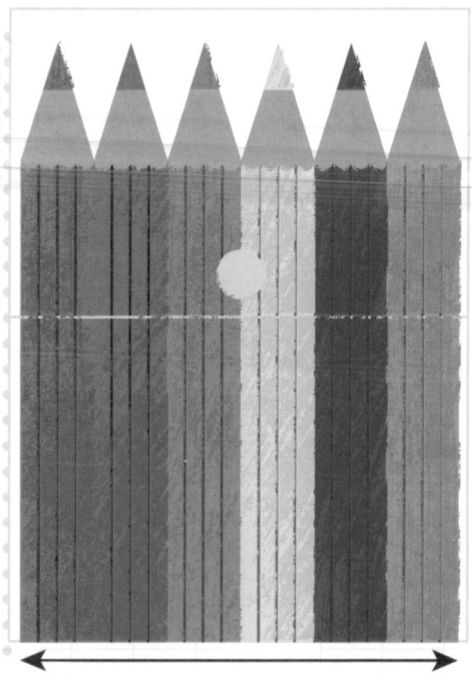

Estimate : _____

Measurement: _____

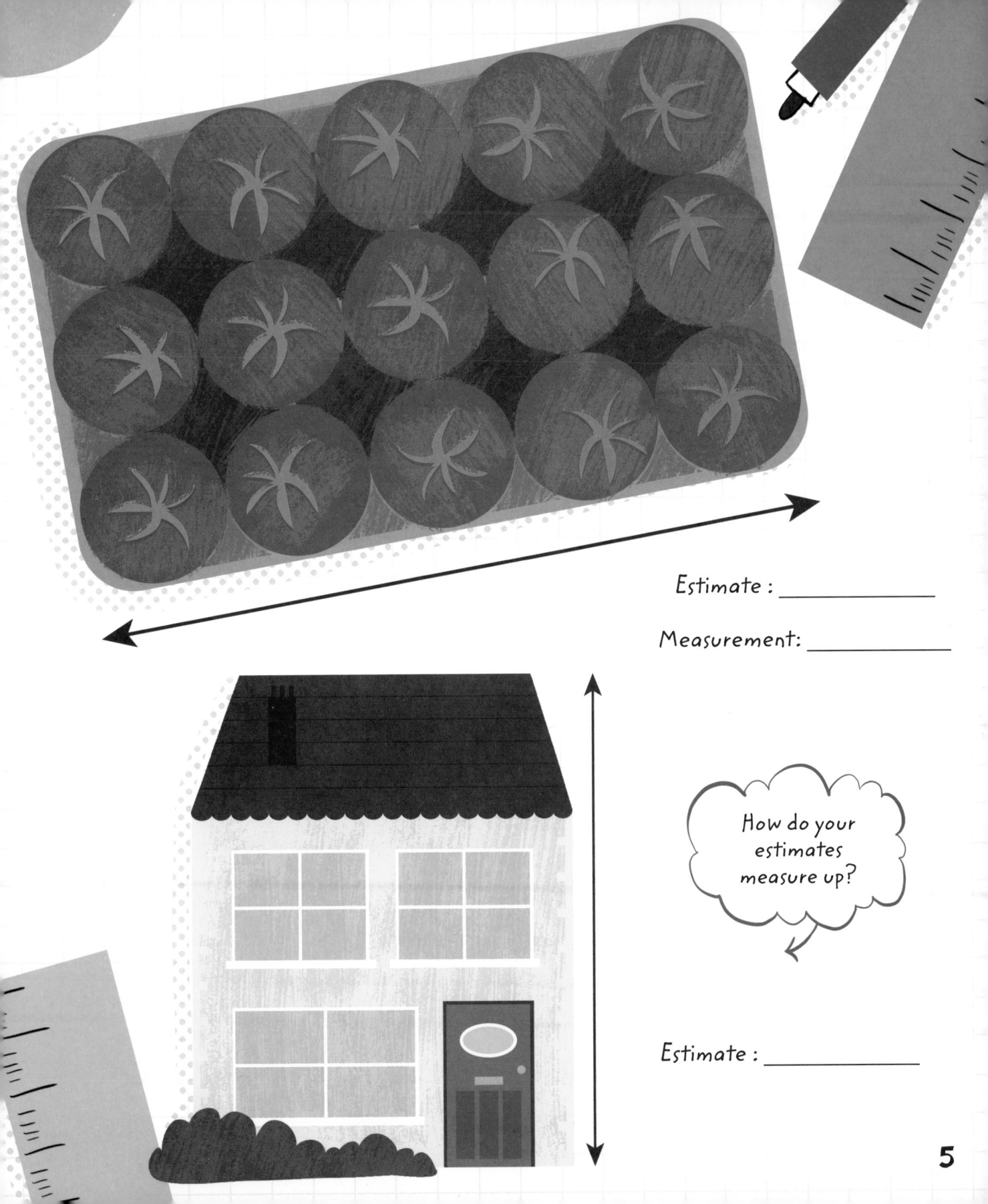
Estimate : _____
Measurement: _____
How do your estimates measure up?
Estimate : _____

SHOPPING

Going shopping involves math! You need to add together your money to check you have enough to buy everything and to give the cashier the right amount.

Check the prices of everything on your shopping list against the money you have in your pocket. On your shopping list, write down how much each will cost and which coins you'll need. Put a cross over each coin when you've used it.
Answers on page 30!

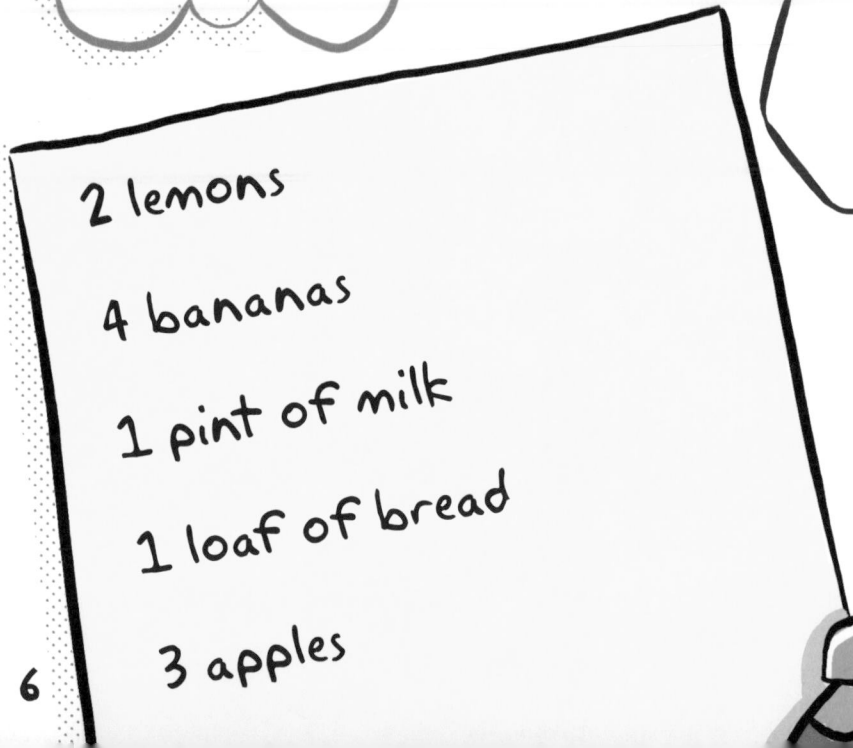

50
a pint
80
OPEN
20 each
25 each
25 each

AT THE POST OFFICE

Bigger things aren't necessarily heavier than smaller things. A pillow filled with feathers is larger than a brick, but the brick is heavier. We can measure weight by using scales, and the metric scale measures in grams (g) and kilograms (kg). There are 1,000 grams in a kilogram.

Check the scales for each of these parcels and write their weights in the spaces provided. Answers on page 30! What do you think is in each box? Draw your answers!

Here are some sample weights to give you ideas. But you can also weigh items around you and choose things to put in the parcels that are not on this list.

Remember this little symbol? ≈

a packet of potato chips ≈ 35g
a tennis ball ≈ 50g
a DVD in its case ≈ 100g
a mobile phone ≈ 150g
a cricket ball ≈ 175g
an exercise book ≈ 200g
a football ≈ 440g
a small bag of sugar ≈ 500g

1.

g

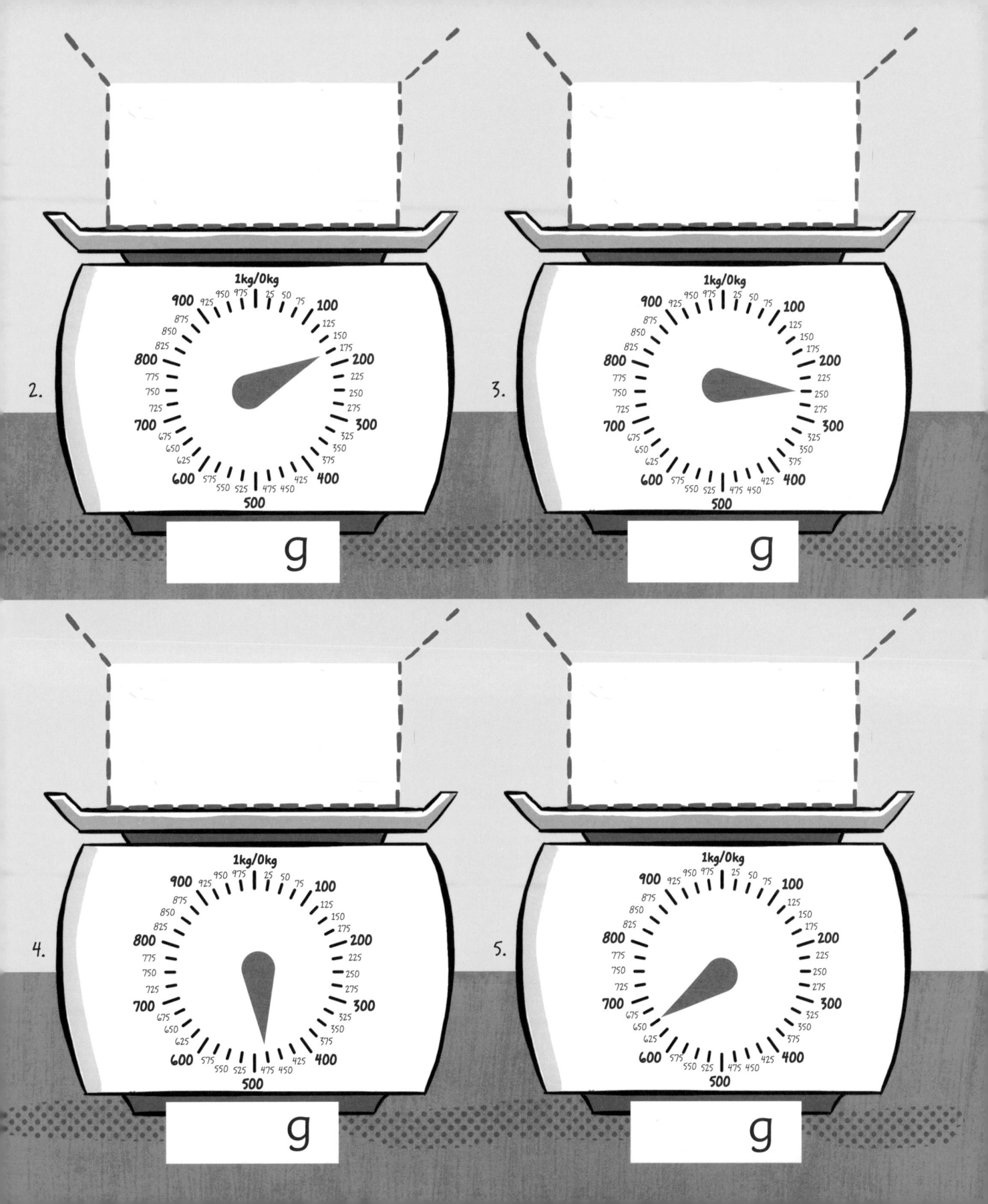
2.
1kg/0kg
900 925 950 975 25 50 75 100 125 150 175 200 225 250 275 300 325 350 375 400 425 450 475 500 525 550 575 600 625 650 675 700 725 750 775 800 825 850 875
g
3.
1kg/0kg
900 925 950 975 25 50 75 100 125 150 175 200 225 250 275 300 325 350 375 400 425 450 475 500 525 550 575 600 625 650 675 700 725 750 775 800 825 850 875
g
4.
1kg/0kg
900 925 950 975 25 50 75 100 125 150 175 200 225 250 275 300 325 350 375 400 425 450 475 500 525 550 575 600 625 650 675 700 725 750 775 800 825 850 875
g
5.
1kg/0kg
900 925 950 975 25 50 75 100 125 150 175 200 225 250 275 300 325 350 375 400 425 450 475 500 525 550 575 600 625 650 675 700 725 750 775 800 825 850 875
g

TAKE AWAYS

Things are taken away—or subtracted—in all sorts of everyday situations. Some things are simple to count, if they are all the same size and shape, such as squares of a chocolate bar. Other things, like liquids, have to be measured in fractions (or equal parts) of a whole unit. The whole unit could be an official way of measuring, such as liters, or anything useful, like a bottle or cup.

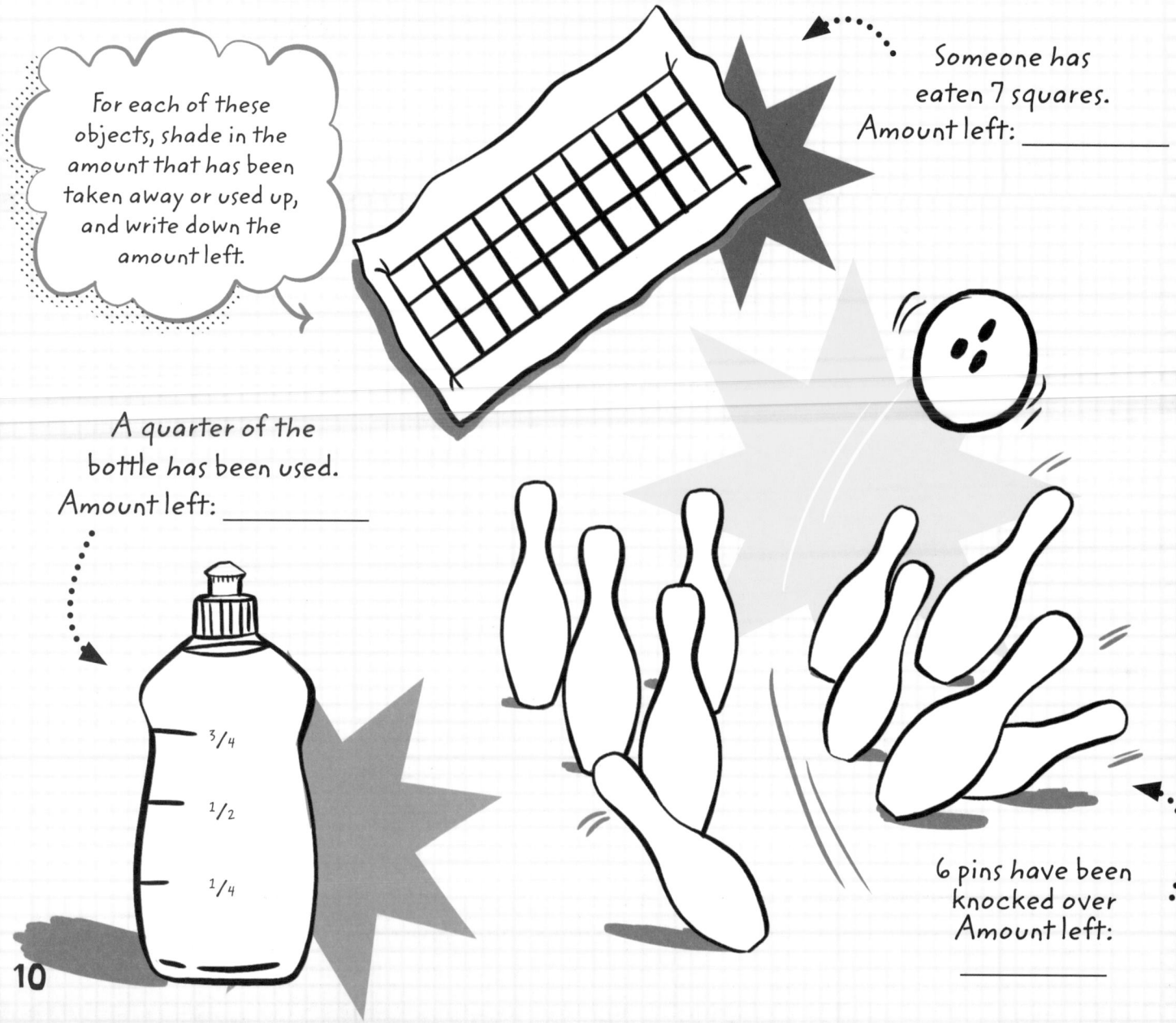

Subtract all the spaces with a dot marked in them by coloring them in—and you'll find a picture revealed in the space left behind.

VOLUME

Capacity—also called "volume"—is a measure of how much space something takes up. You can measure the capacity of things that can be poured from one container to another. Capacity can be measured in milliliters (ml) and liters (l), and there are 1,000 milliliters in a liter. However, you might see capacity measured in all sorts of ways.

Here are some common ways capacity is measured:

In this recipe, some of the ingredients are measured in weight, and some are measured in volume. Circle the words that are telling you what volume to use.

Clue: Remember—volume isn't always measured in just milliliters and liters.

Vanilla cupcakes

4 oz. / 110g butter
4 oz. / 110g caster sugar
2 free-range eggs
1 teaspoon vanilla extract
4 oz. / 110g self-raising flour
1-2 tablespoons milk

Buttercream icing

5 oz. / 140g butter
9 3/4 oz. / 280g icing sugar
1-2 tablespoons milk
a few drops food coloring

1. Preheat the oven to 180° C (350° F) and line a muffin tin with paper cases (ask an adult to help you).

2. Cream the butter and sugar together then slowly beat in the eggs and vanilla extract.

3. Carefully mix in the flour adding little drops of milk as you go.

4. Bake for 10-15 minutes until golden on top then leave to cool.

5. Beat the butter for the icing until soft then add half of the icing sugar and beat some more.

6. Add the rest of the icing sugar and the milk to the butter and mix until smooth.

7. Decorate your cupcakes! Use food coloring in the icing for a special finish.

MULTIPLES

Multiplication is adding the same number to itself an amount of times. So, 3 x 3 means to add 3 to itself three times, or 3 + 3 + 3.

You can represent 3 x 3 in a grid, too, where there are 3 rows and 3 columns, like this:

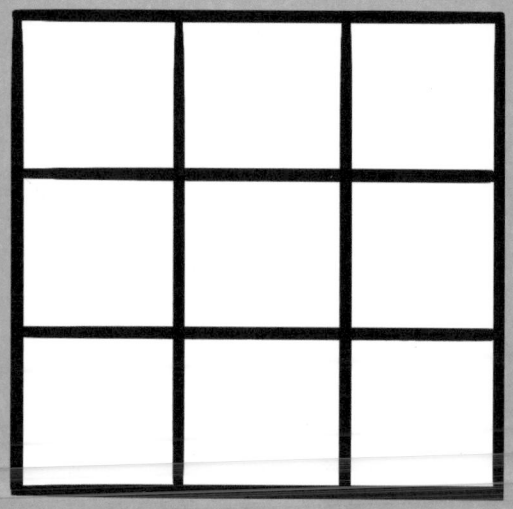

or 2 x 4 like this:

And counting the number of squares gives you the answer to the question.

Use the pictures opposite to help you solve these multiplication questions.
Look for the boxes that match the number of rows and columns in the question.

2 X 5 =		5 X 6 =	
3 X 6 =		8 X 9 =	
4 X 5 =		9 X 10 =	

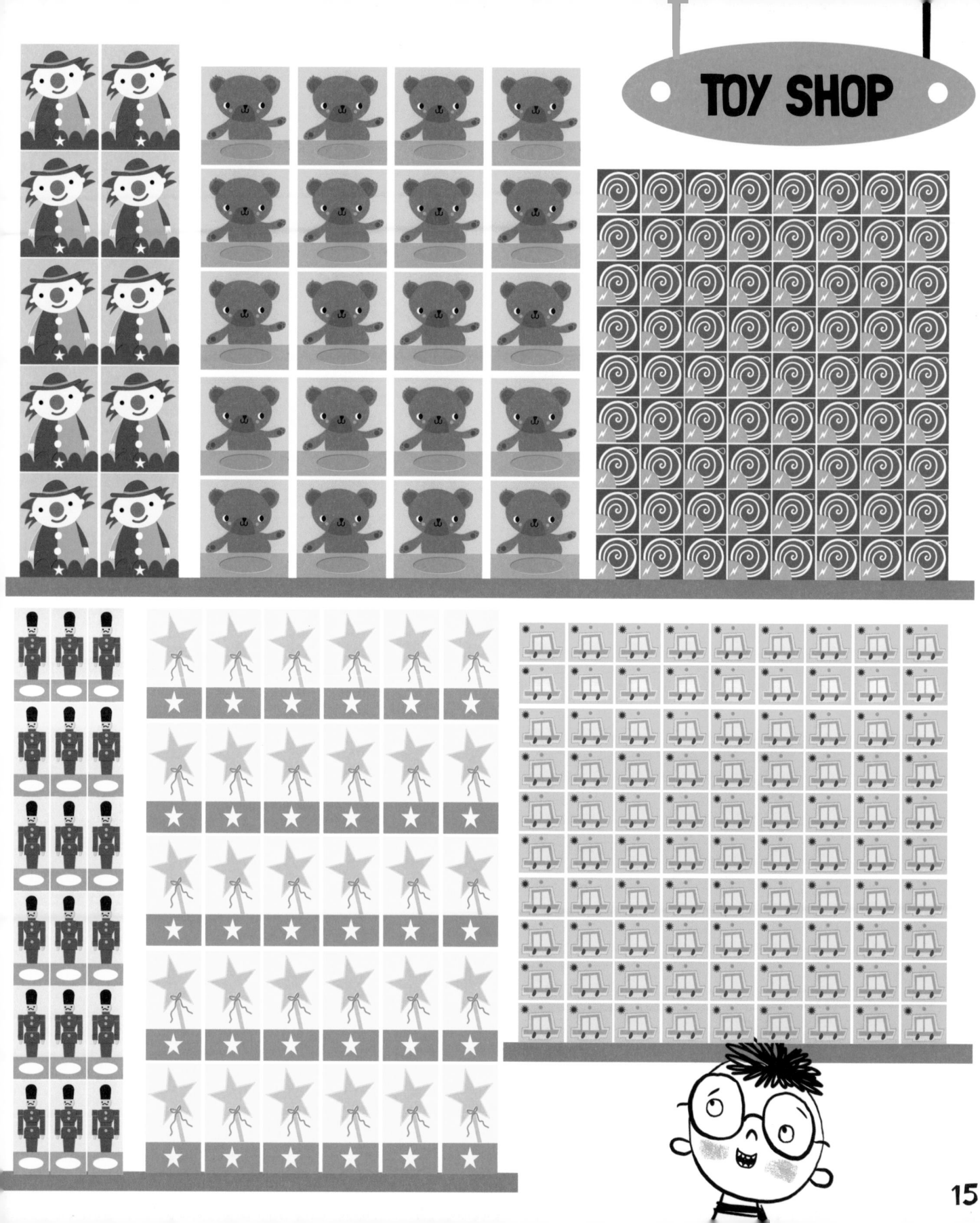
TOY SHOP

RACING MATH

It's important to know how to measure time. Telling the time helps you arrive at school on time and helps your teacher make sure your lessons last the right amount of time. People running races also need to measure time to know exactly how long they have taken. Time can be measured in seconds, minutes and hours. There are 60 seconds in a minute and 60 minutes in an hour.

Ahmed
- 10 seconds
Betty
- 5 seconds
1st : Ahmed
2nd : Betty
3rd : Caden 1 minute 5 seconds
4th : Daniel
5th : Evie

SHARING

Sharing things out is called "division." Things can be shared out evenly but sometimes there will be leftovers known as the remainder.

These cakes have all been cut into different numbers of slices. First, count the number of slices, then use different colored pencils to share out the slices equally amongst the number of guests listed for each cake. Each guest can have more than one slice of cake but they must all have the same number of slices each. Here's one to start you off.

Number of slices: 8
Share between 4 guests
Slices left over: 0

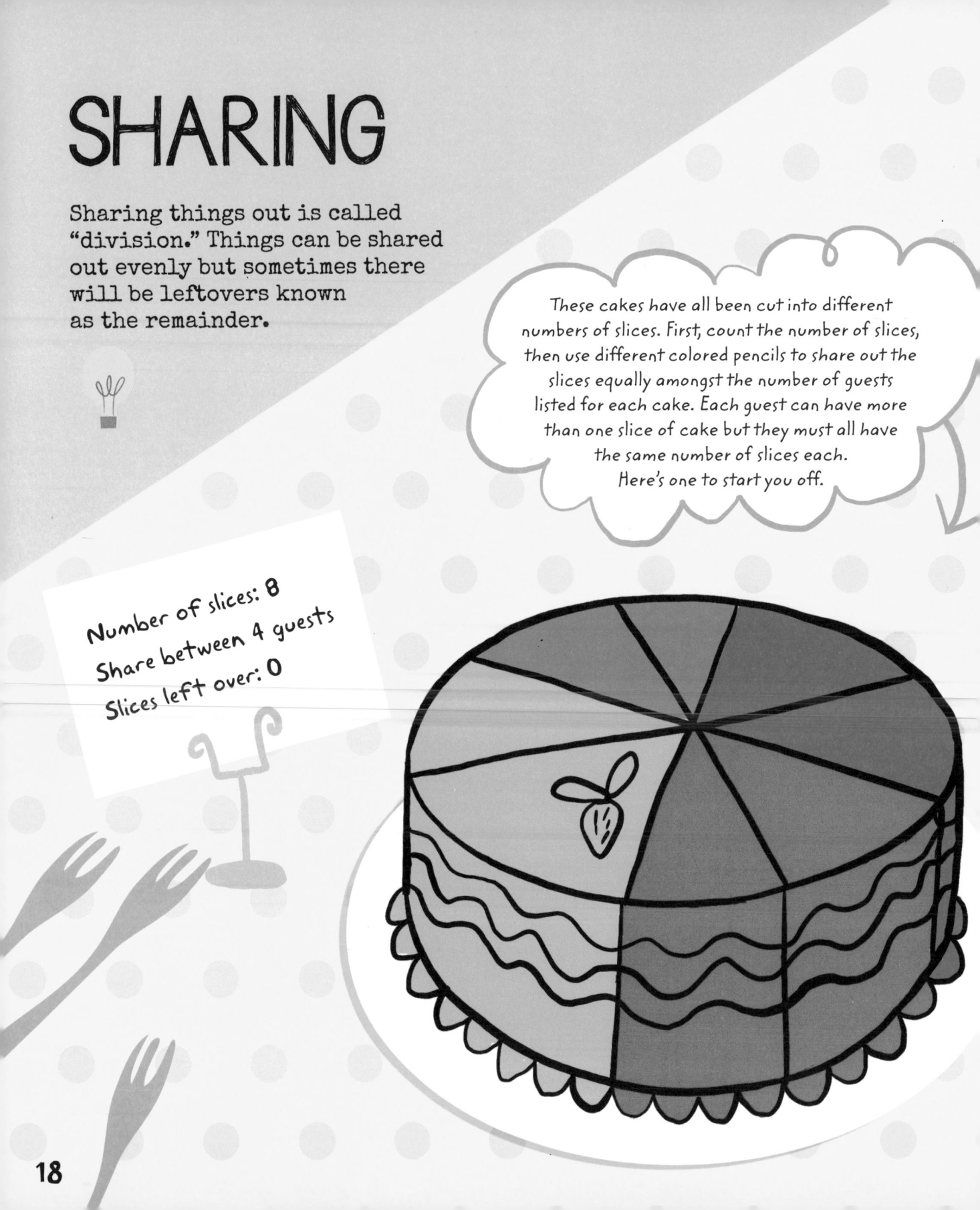

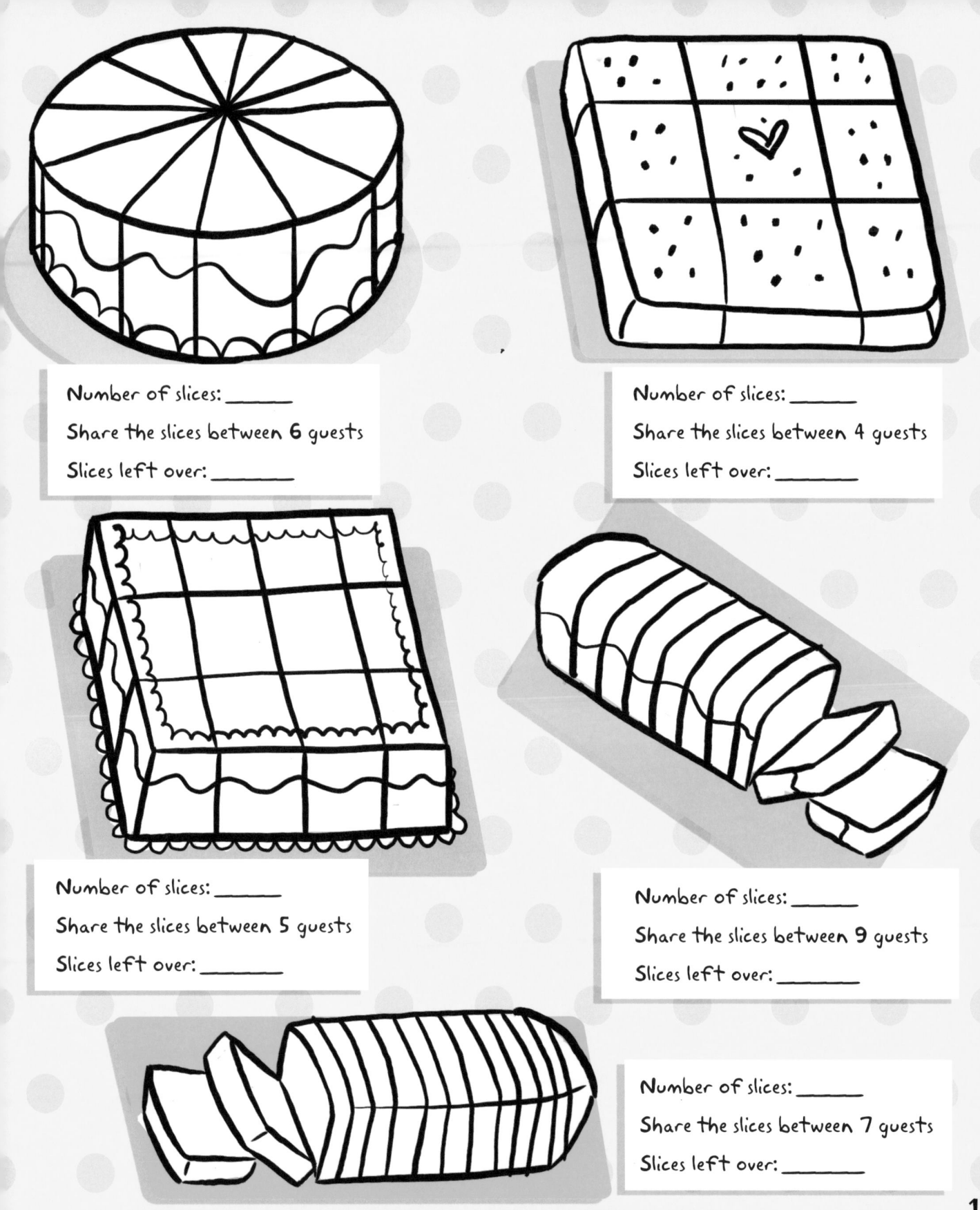

Number of slices: _____

Share the slices between 6 guests

Slices left over: _____

Number of slices: _____

Share the slices between 4 guests

Slices left over: _____

Number of slices: _____

Share the slices between 5 guests

Slices left over: _____

Number of slices: _____

Share the slices between 9 guests

Slices left over: _____

Number of slices: _____

Share the slices between 7 guests

Slices left over: _____

CODE BREAKER

Codes are used to hide information. The important part is the key, which helps you decipher the code. There are many different ways to write code. Some are quite famous, but the hardest to crack are the ones that are made up specially with secret rules that only a very small number of people know.

Here are some famous codes. For each one, use the key to decode the secret messages.

THE REVERSE ALPHABET

The clue's in the title! The code is simply the reverse of the alphabet. This code is easy to crack but that also means you'll never forget how to crack it, even if you lose your key.

A	B	C	D	E	F	G	H	I	J	K	L	M	N	O	P	Q	R	S	T	U	V	W	X	Y	Z
Z	Y	X	W	V	U	T	S	R	Q	P	O	N	M	L	K	J	I	H	G	F	E	D	C	B	A

D	S	Z	G		R	H		U	L	I		W	R	M	M	V	I	?

AUGUSTUS'S CODE

Another simple code, this time the alphabet is all shifted on one place, so that A=B, B=C, and so on until Z=A. This message uses the bottom line of the code.

A	B	C	D	E	F	G	H	I	J	K	L	M	N	O	P	Q	R	S	T	U	V	W	X	Y	Z
Z	A	B	C	D	E	F	G	H	I	J	K	L	M	N	O	P	Q	R	S	T	U	V	W	X	Y

Z	T	F	T	R	S	T	R		V	Z	R		Z		Q	N	L	Z	M

PICTOGRAM CODE

You don't always need to use letters in your code!
Pictograms, or little pictures, can take the place of letters.

A	B	C	D	E	F	G	H	I	J	K	L	M	N	O	P	Q	R	S	T	U	V	W	X	Y	Z
✌	👌	👍	👎	👈	👉	☝	👆	✋	☺	😐	☹	💣	☠	⚑	⚐	✈	☼	💧	❄	✝	✞	✠	✠	✡	☪

✋	💧		❄	👆	✋	💧		👈	✌	💧	✡		⚐	☼		👆	✌	☼	👎	?

Have a go at making your own code.
Fill in the empty boxes to give each letter a code, and then use your code to write a secret message! Don't forget to share the code with a partner so they can decipher your message.

A	B	C	D	E	F	G

H	I	J	K	L	M	N

O	P	Q	R	S	T	U

V	W	X	Y	Z

TURN THE TABLES

Making notes of the things we see can help us to see patterns. Writing stuff down helps us to take more notice.

Look at this scene and record information about it in the table by putting ticks in the right boxes. The first line has been filled in for you.

	Mum	Dad	brother	sister	baby
eating cereal			✓	✓	✓
eating toast					
curly hair					
straight hair					
wearing red					
smiling					
drinking juice					
drinking milk					

BAR CHARTS

Tables gather numbers in a grid. Bar charts are a fun way to turn information into something visual. A "bar" on the chart represents the number value in the table.

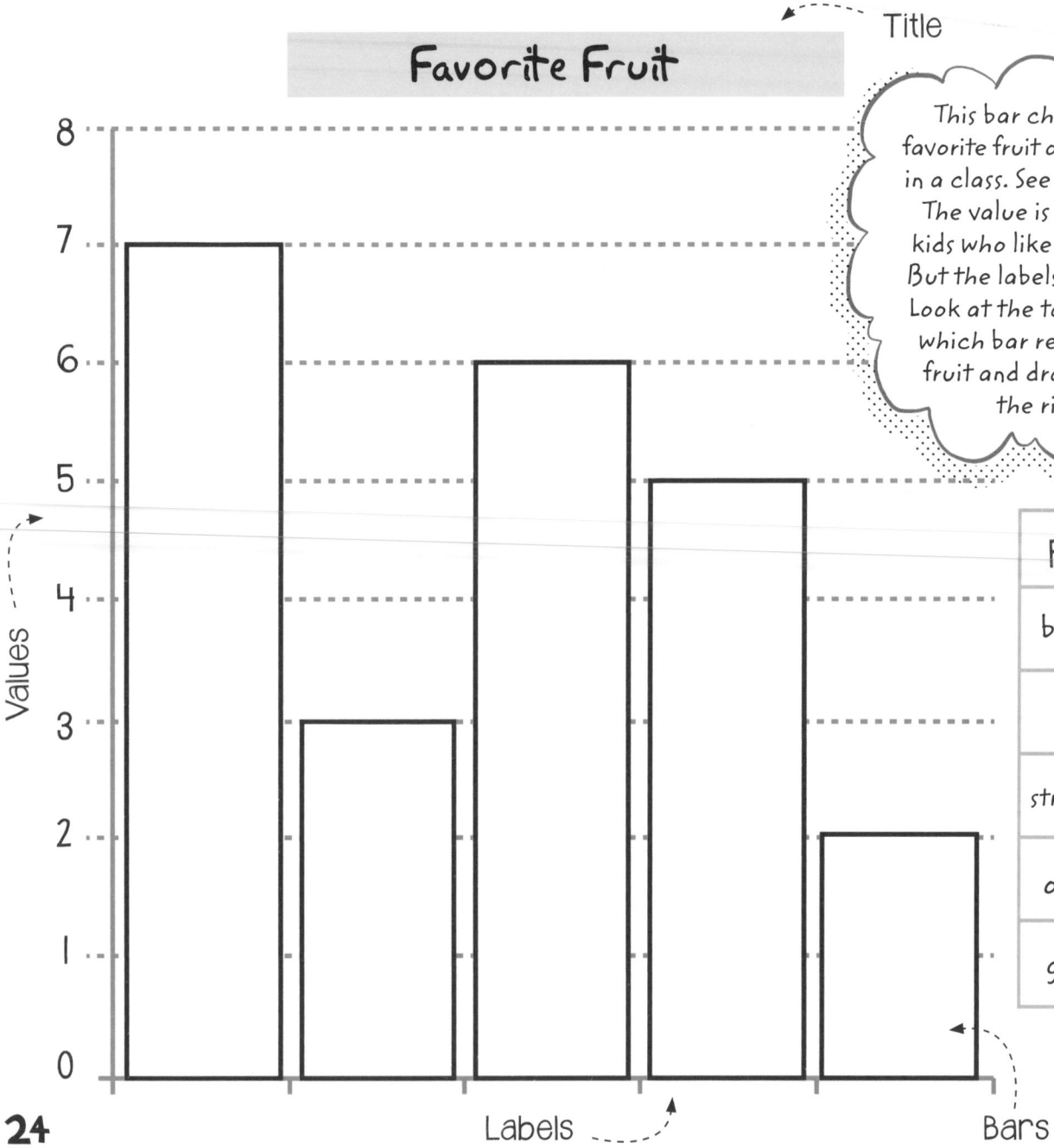

This bar chart shows the favorite fruit of all the children in a class. See the table below. The value is the number of kids who like each fruit best. But the labels have vanished! Look at the table to work out which bar represents which fruit and draw the fruit on the right bar.

Fruit	Value
banana	6
apple	7
strawberry	5
orange	2
grapes	3

Victor gathered this information about his friends' favorite hobbies. Use a pencil and ruler to turn the information in this table into a bar chart.

Hobby	Value
football	8
ballet	4
swimming	5
karate	2
scouts	5

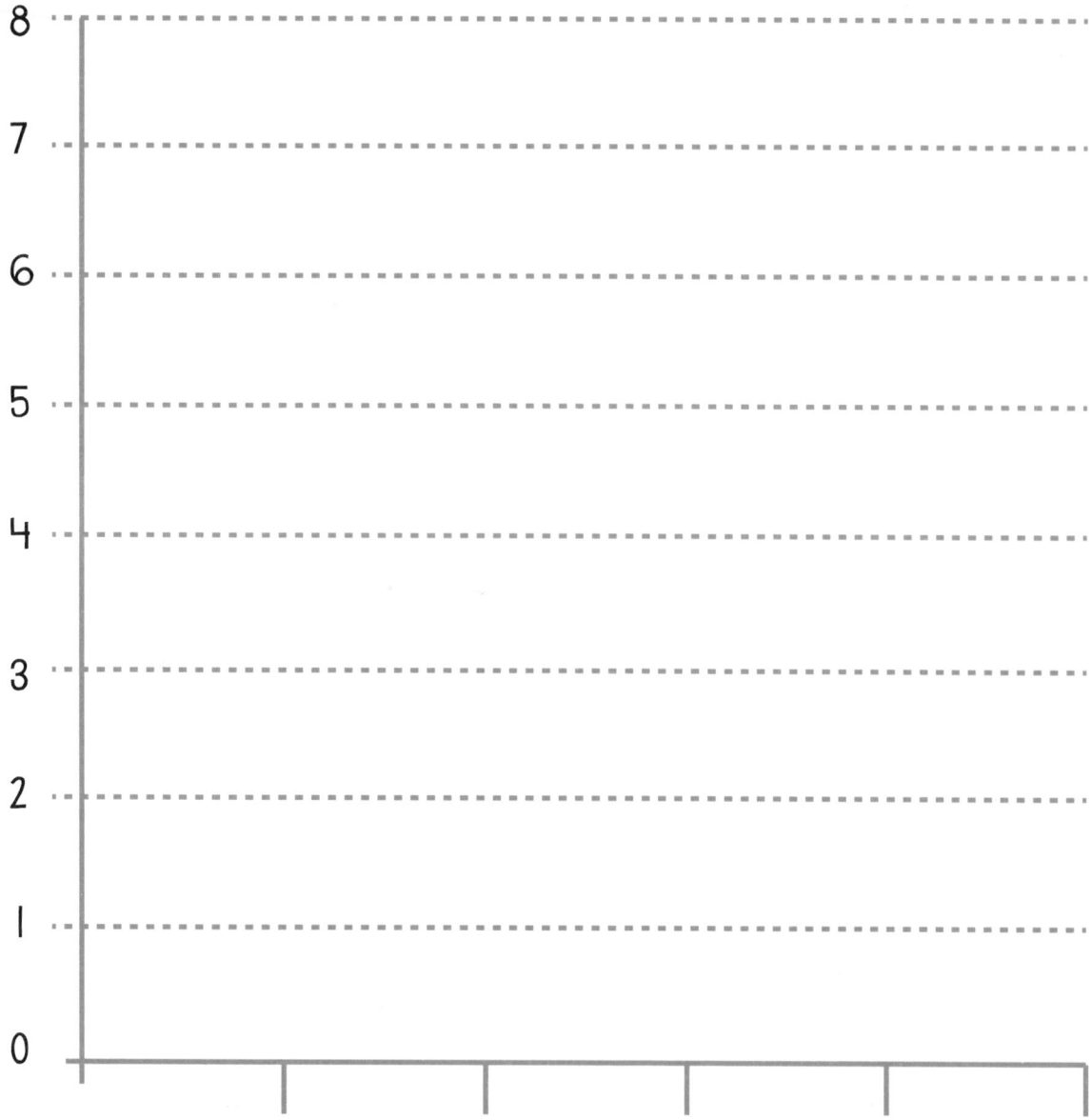

RIGHT ANGLES

When two straight lines meet they make an angle. A "right angle" is a special kind of angle, shaped like an "L"—once you can recognize a right angle you'll see they are all around us.

ROUNDING UP

Sometimes it's easier to understand larger numbers if they are rounded up or down to something simpler.

Numbers 1 to 4 are rounded down to the nearest 0. So 13 becomes 10.

Numbers 5 to 9 are rounded up to the nearest 0. So 27 becomes 30.

You can also round off numbers and use other words to describe numbers. Here are some words you can use to describe a number without saying the exact number.

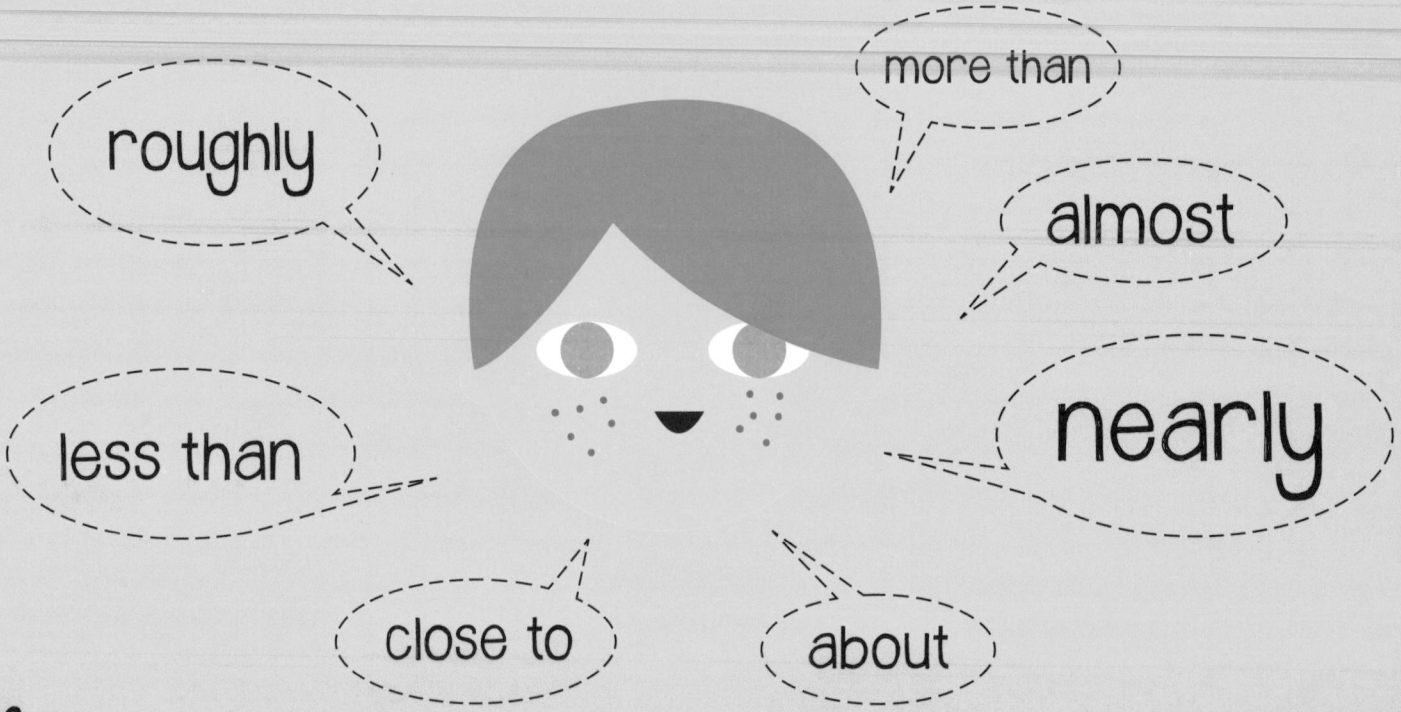

In these conversations, reply to the friend talking in exact numbers with another way of describing the number, rounded off. Use the words suggested on the opposite page to help you.
I have 97 action figures!
You have nearly 100 action figures!
I can skip 32 times without stopping!
I am 8 years and 11 months old.
I scored a basket 11 times in a row!
There are 26 pupils in my class.

ANSWERS

Pages 4-5

Pencils
Estimate : **6 cm**
Measurement : **6.3 cm**

Punnet of cherry tomatoes
Estimate : **15 cm**
Measurement : **15.3 cm**

House
Estimate : **6 m**

Pages 6-7

2 lemons = 40 (2 x 20)

4 bananas = $1 (1 x $1)

1 pint of milk = 50 (1 x 50)

1 loaf of bread = 80 (1 x 50, 1 x 20, 1 x 10)

3 apples = 75 (1 x 50, 2 x 10, 1 x 5)

Page 8-9

Here are the weights showing on the scales and some ideas for what could be inside the parcels. You might have chosen other things to go in the parcels by weighing items around you.

1. The scale shows 100g = a DVD in its case
2. The scale shows 175g = a cricket ball
3. The scale shows 250g = an exercise book + a tennis ball
4. The scale shows 475g = a football + a packet of crisps
5. The scale shows 650g = a small bag of sugar + a mobile phone

Page 10

Chocolate bar	Bottle of laundry liquid	Bowling pins
Amount left: 23	**Amount left: 3/4**	**Amount left: 4**

Page 22-23

Reverse Alphabet: What is for dinner?

Augustus's Code: Augustus was a Roman

Pictogram Code: Is this easy or hard?

Page 22-23

	Mum	Dad	brother	sister	baby
eating cereal			✓	✓	✓
eating toast	✓		✓		
curly hair	✓		✓		
straight hair		✓		✓	
wearing red	✓	✓			✓
smiling	✓		✓		✓
drinking juice			✓	✓	
drinking milk					✓

Page 26-27

There are 8 right angles in the picture.

Page 24-25

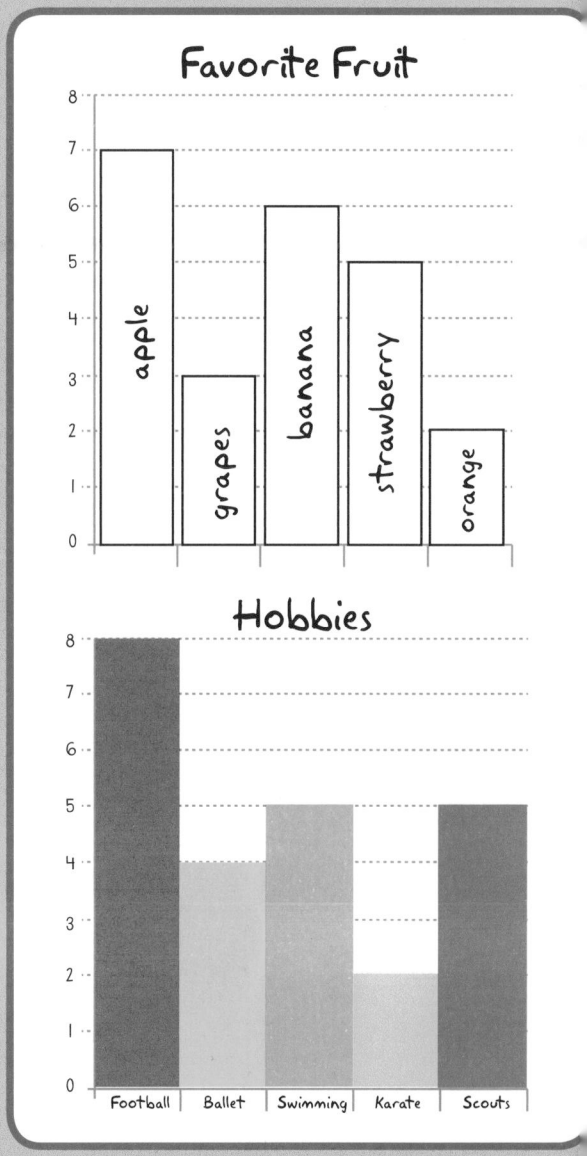

Page 28-29

Possible answers:

- You can skip more than 30 times!
- You are nearly 9 years old.
- You have scored more than 10 baskets in a row.
- You have close to 30 pupils in your class.

Page 11

Page 12

Vanilla cupcakes

4 oz. / 110g butter

4 oz. / 110g caster sugar

2 free-range eggs

1 teaspoon vanilla extract

4 oz. / 110g self-raising flour

1-2 tablespoons milk

Buttercream icing

5 oz. / 140g butter

9 3/4 oz. / 280g icing sugar

1-2 tablespoons milk

a few drops food coloring

Page 14-15

2 X 5 = 10
3 X 6 = 18
4 X 5 = 20
5 X 6 = 30
8 X 9 = 72
9 X 10 = 90

Page 16-17

1st : Ahmed 55 seconds
2nd : Betty 1 minute
3rd : Caden 1 minute 5 seconds
4th : Daniel 1 minute 12 seconds
5th : Evie 1 minute 17 seconds

Page 18-19

Cake 1
Number of slices: 12
Slices left over: 0

Cake 2
Number of slices: 9
Slices left over: 1

Cake 3
Number of slices: 12
Slices left over: 2

Cake 4
Number of slices: 10
Slices left over: 1

Cake 5
Number of slices: 14
Slices left over: 0